UNEARTHING LEGACIES

A Guide to Tracing American Indian Ancestry

Penelope Green

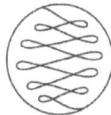

GLOBAL
PUBLISHING
SOLUTIONS

UNEARTHING LEGACIES: A GUIDE TO TRACING AMERICAN INDIAN ANCESTRY

Published by Global Publishing Solutions, LLC
923 Fieldside Drive
Matteson, Illinois 60443
www.globalpublishingsolutions.com

Library of Congress Control Number
2023945625
International Standard Book Number
ISBN: 979-8-9886045-6-3
E-book International Standard Book Number:
979-8-9886045-7-0

Printed in the United States of America

TABLE OF CONTENTS

INTRODUCTION: EMBRACING ANCESTRAL ECHOES

In "Unearthing Legacies: A Guide to Tracing American Indian Ancestry," we embark on a voyage that is both a celebration and a challenge—an exploration of roots that extends beyond names and dates, delving into the cultural nuances and historical complexities that define American Indian genealogy. My aim is to offer you a compass, a lantern, and a map through the uncharted territories of indigenous heritage research.

The journey to trace American Indian ancestry is often marked by unique hurdles, as historical records, tribal affiliations, and cultural dynamics have woven intricate patterns. However, within these challenges lie opportunities to connect with narratives of resilience, adaptability, and a steadfast connection to the land. Through the wisdom of oral histories, the threads of written records, and the pathways of DNA, we'll navigate these complexities, uncovering the profound stories of those who walked before us.

This guide extends an invitation to traverse the trails of oral traditions, navigate the labyrinths of documentation, and embrace the complexities of tribal identities. We'll examine the nuances of cultural sensitivity and ethical considerations, recognizing that this journey is not just about uncovering facts—it's about fostering connections, understanding legacies, and honoring ancestral contributions.

Together, we'll explore the intricacies of American Indian genealogy with respect and reverence. As we peer into the past, we do so with a recognition that our quest shapes not only our own understanding but also contributes to the mosaic of history that has shaped and continues to shape our collective identity.

So, with an open heart and a curious spirit, let us embark on this expedition of discovery. May the stories of your ancestors guide you, and may the knowledge gained in these pages be a lantern illuminating the path of your American Indian heritage, connecting you to the wisdom of generations past and the limitless potential of generations to come.

CHARTING THE COURSE: NAVIGATING THE COMPLEXITIES OF AMERICAN INDIAN GENEALOGY

Introduction

Tracing American Indian ancestry is a voyage that requires not only research skills but also a deep understanding of historical contexts, cultural dynamics, and the unique challenges faced by indigenous communities. In this chapter, we set sail by exploring the intricate terrain of American Indian genealogy and preparing to navigate the complexities that lie ahead.

A Historical Landscape of Complexity

1. **Colonial Encounters**: Understand the impact of European colonization on indigenous communities and the subsequent disruptions to ancestral connections and records.
2. **Tribal Diversity**: Recognize the vast diversity of American Indian tribes, each with distinct histories, languages, and cultural practices.

The Oral Tradition: A Pillar of Heritage

1. **Oral Histories**: Explore the importance of oral traditions in American Indian culture, passing down stories and knowledge through generations.

2. **Unearthing Stories**: Learn how to engage with elders and family members to gather oral histories and preserve the wisdom of the past.

Documenting the Undocumented

1. **Limited Records**: Acknowledge the scarcity of written records for American Indian genealogy due to historical factors and government policies.
2. **Agency Records**: Discover the significance of records created by government agencies, such as the Bureau of Indian Affairs, for tracing ancestry.

Naming Conventions and Identity

1. **Naming Traditions**: Understand the significance of American Indian naming practices and the challenges of name changes imposed by external forces.
2. **Identity Shifts**: Explore how shifting identities due to historical events and cultural assimilation impact genealogical research.

Tribal Sovereignty and Citizenship

1. **Sovereign Nations**: Grasp the concept of tribal sovereignty and its influence on genealogical research and tribal citizenship.
2. **Enrollment Processes**: Navigate the complexities of tribal enrollment criteria, blood quantum requirements, and the implications for ancestral recognition.

Challenges of Modernity

1. **Urban Relocation**: Understand the impact of urbanization and relocation policies on indigenous communities and genealogical connections.
2. **Loss of Connection**: Address the challenge of maintaining cultural ties and genealogical knowledge in the face of urbanization and assimilation.

A Path Forward: Compassion and Respect

1. **Cultural Sensitivity**: Embrace cultural sensitivity as a guiding principle in American Indian genealogy, honoring traditions and protecting sacred knowledge.
2. **Collaborative Approach**: Recognize the importance of collaborating with tribal members and communities, approaching genealogy as a shared endeavor.

Navigating the complexities of American Indian genealogy requires a blend of historical awareness, cultural sensitivity, and meticulous research. As we set sail on this exploration, remember that the journey is not solely about discovering names and dates—it's about weaving together stories, preserving legacies, and forging connections that transcend time. With each chapter of this journey, we inch closer to uncovering the hidden gems of American Indian ancestry and celebrating the vibrant tapestry of indigenous heritage.

LISTENING TO ANCESTRAL WHISPERS: WALKING THROUGH THE TRAIL OF ORAL HISTORIES AND TRADITIONS

Introduction

Oral histories and traditions play a vital role in American Indian communities. Green guides readers in capturing and deciphering family stories, oral traditions, and tribal narratives to uncover hidden threads of ancestral connections.

In the annals of American Indian genealogy, the echoes of the past resonate most vividly through oral histories and traditions. Passed down through generations, these narratives hold the power to illuminate the lives, experiences, and connections of our ancestors. In this chapter, we embark on a journey guided by the whispers of oral traditions, learning to decode their messages and uncover hidden threads of ancestral identity.

Tales of Timeless Wisdom

1. **The Role of Oral Tradition**: Understand the integral role of oral histories as a conduit for preserving cultural knowledge and ancestral stories.

2. **Generational Narratives**: Explore how oral histories bridge the gap between generations, carrying the wisdom and experiences of the past into the present.

Capturing Family Stories

1. **Interviewing Elders**: Learn techniques for respectfully engaging with elders and family members to capture their memories and narratives.
2. **Listening with Empathy**: Embrace active listening and empathy to create a safe and supportive environment for sharing personal stories.

Interpreting Oral Traditions

1. **Symbolism and Metaphor**: Recognize that oral traditions often employ symbolism, metaphor, and allegory to convey deeper meanings.
2. **Cultural Context**: Contextualize oral narratives within the cultural framework of the tribe or community, understanding their significance.

Weaving the Threads of Connection

1. **Family Genealogies**: Discover how family genealogies are interwoven with oral traditions, anchoring individuals within the broader ancestral context.
2. **Relating to the Land**: Understand how oral histories connect to the land, conveying ties to specific places and the natural world.

Navigating the Challenges

1. **Fragmentation of Stories**: Address the challenges of fragmented stories and variations in oral traditions due to the passage of time and external influences.
2. **Validation and Corroboration**: Learn techniques for validating oral histories through cross-referencing with other sources and accounts.

Preserving for Posterity

1. **Recording and Documentation**: Explore methods for recording oral histories, whether through audio, video, transcription, or written narratives.
2. **Ethical Considerations**: Consider ethical considerations when sharing oral histories, respecting the wishes and privacy of storytellers.

Sharing and Celebrating

1. **Passing the Torch**: Encourage the sharing of oral histories with younger generations to ensure their preservation for the future.
2. **Community Engagement**: Engage with tribal and local communities to contribute to the collective preservation of oral traditions.

As we navigate the trail of oral histories and traditions, we walk alongside the voices of our ancestors, learning to interpret their messages and honor their experiences. Each story shared, each memory recounted, adds another layer to the vibrant tapestry of American Indian heritage. By listening with open hearts and embracing the teachings of our forebears, we connect not only with our own lineage but also with the enduring legacy of indigenous cultures that have shaped the land and the soul of this nation.

UNRAVELING THE DOCUMENTATION DILEMMA: DOCUMENTING THE UNDOCUMENTED

Introduction

In the pursuit of tracing American Indian ancestry, the scarcity of written records can present a formidable challenge. Historical events, government policies, and the transient nature of indigenous communities have contributed to a dearth of documentation. In this chapter, we delve into the strategies and resources that enable us to uncover the hidden fragments of ancestral history and piece together a more complete narrative.

Agency Records: A Window into the Past

1. **Bureau of Indian Affairs Records**: Explore the significance of records created by the Bureau of Indian Affairs, including enrollment records, land allotment files, and census data.
2. **Dawes Rolls and Guion Miller Rolls**: Understand the role of these rolls in documenting individuals of American Indian descent for the purpose of land allotment and reparations.

School Records and Mission Documents

1. **Boarding Schools**: Investigate the impact of boarding schools on indigenous communities and access records from these institutions that may hold information about individuals and families.
2. **Mission Records**: Examine records created by religious missions that established contact with American Indian communities, including baptismal and marriage records.

Local and State Archives

1. **County Records**: Explore local county records, including birth, marriage, and death records, as well as land and probate records that can shed light on familial connections.
2. **State Archives**: Investigate state-level archives for resources such as vital records, historical newspapers, and land ownership documents.

Church Registers and Baptismal Records

1. **Sacramental Records**: Recognize the value of church registers and baptismal records in documenting American Indian individuals through religious ceremonies.
2. **Baptismal Names**: Understand how baptisms often resulted in the assignment of Christian names, which may differ from traditional indigenous names.

Wills, Probate, and Land Records

1. **Estate Documents**: Explore wills and probate records for insights into familial relationships, inheritance, and land ownership.
2. **Land Allotments**: Investigate the allocation of land to American Indian individuals and families, which can provide clues about their presence and affiliations.

Challenges of Fragmented Records

1. **Intergenerational Disconnection**: Address how fragmented records can result from historical events, migration, and the dislocation of families.
2. **Overcoming Roadblocks**: Learn strategies for navigating gaps in records, exploring alternate sources, and cross-referencing information.

Harnessing Digital Resources

1. **Online Databases**: Explore digital archives, repositories, and websites that offer searchable collections of American Indian-related records.
2. **Collaborative Efforts**: Discover genealogy projects and collaborative initiatives that aim to digitize, index, and share historical documents.

As we sift through the fragments of the past, each record uncovered adds a layer of understanding to the story of American Indian ancestry. While the challenge of limited documentation is real, the resilience of our communities and the collaborative efforts of researchers and historians continue to bring fragments into focus. By piecing together these fragments, we honor the lives of those who walked before us and contribute to the vibrant tapestry of indigenous heritage.

TRIBAL IDENTITY AND ANCESTRAL RECOGNITION: NAVIGATING SOVEREIGNTY AND CITIZENSHIP

Introduction

The intricate web of tribal identity lies at the heart of American Indian genealogy. Tribes possess distinct histories, languages, and cultural practices, each weaving a unique thread into the fabric of indigenous heritage. In this chapter, we delve into the complexities of tribal sovereignty, enrollment processes, and the journey to affirm one's connection to a tribal community.

Tribal Sovereignty and Self-Determination

1. **Sovereign Nations**: Understand the concept of tribal sovereignty as the inherent right of indigenous nations to govern themselves and make decisions about their communities.

2. **Cultural Autonomy**: Explore how tribal sovereignty extends to cultural practices, land management, and preservation of ancestral knowledge.

Tribal Enrollment Criteria

1. **Defining Membership**: Recognize that tribes determine their own criteria for enrollment, which can include lineage, blood quantum, residency, and other factors.
2. **Challenges of Inclusion**: Understand that membership criteria can lead to challenges of exclusion for individuals who don't meet specific requirements.

Blood Quantum: A Double-Edged Measure

1. **Blood Quantum Calculation**: Learn about the concept of blood quantum, a measure of an individual's indigenous ancestry, and how it's calculated.
2. **Critiques and Debates**: Explore the debates surrounding blood quantum, including concerns about cultural preservation and identity.

Dual Enrollment and Citizenship

1. **Dual Enrollment**: Discover the complexities faced by individuals who may be eligible for enrollment in multiple tribes due to intertribal marriages.
2. **Tribal Citizenship**: Understand that tribal enrollment is not only a matter of genealogy but also of establishing

connections with the community and contributing to its well-being.

Documenting Tribal Affiliation

1. **Tribal Enrollment Records**: Learn how to access tribal enrollment records and understand the information they provide about family relationships and affiliations.
2. **Affiliation Letters**: Explore the role of affiliation letters, which may be required to establish connections to a specific tribe.

Maintaining Cultural Ties

1. **Cultural Continuity**: Recognize that tribal membership is often tied to maintaining cultural connections, language, and involvement in tribal activities.
2. **Cultural Contributions**: Understand that the recognition of tribal citizenship often comes with responsibilities to contribute to the well-being of the community.

Ethics of Enrollment and Identity

1. **Respect for Sovereignty**: Embrace the principle of respecting tribal sovereignty and recognizing that decisions about enrollment belong to the tribal community.

2. **Ethical Considerations**: Navigate the ethical considerations of seeking tribal enrollment, including the potential impact on the tribal community.

Challenges and Rewards of Affiliation

1. **Fulfillment of Connection**: Acknowledge the emotional significance of gaining tribal affiliation, reconnecting with ancestral roots, and contributing to tribal legacies.

2. **Family and Community Bonds**: Understand that tribal affiliation extends beyond an individual's genealogy, encompassing connections to extended family and the wider community.

Navigating the intricacies of tribal identity and enrollment requires sensitivity, respect, and an appreciation for the diversity of indigenous cultures. As we explore the pathways to tribal citizenship, we recognize that the journey is about more than proving lineage—it's about honoring cultural traditions, embracing community, and contributing to the ongoing narrative of American Indian heritage.

FROM CENSUS TO CONNECTION: OVERCOMING CENSUS OBSTACLES

Introduction

The census, a tool often used in genealogy research, presents its own set of challenges when tracing American Indian ancestry. Misclassification, underreporting, and inconsistent categorization have obscured the presence of indigenous populations. In this chapter, we embark on a journey to decipher the census data, unveiling the stories hidden within demographic records.

Census as Historical Snapshots

1. **Census Records Overview**: Understand the role of census records as snapshots of populations at specific points in time, providing valuable demographic insights.
2. **Census Intervals**: Explore the census intervals from 1790 onward and their significance in tracking changes within American Indian communities.

Census Challenges and Indigenous Populations

1. **Misclassification and Underreporting**: Recognize the challenges posed by misclassification of race and the

tendency for American Indian populations to be underrepresented.

2. **Categorization Changes**: Understand how changes in census categories over time impact the identification and enumeration of indigenous populations.

Tribal Listings and Community Designations

1. **Tribal Enumeration**: Learn about census years that included special schedules for American Indian populations and how tribal affiliations were recorded.

2. **Community Designations**: Explore the designations of "Indian Reservations" and "Indian Colonies" and their implications for census data analysis.

Interpreting Enumeration Districts

1. **Urban and Rural Contexts**: Differentiate between urban and rural enumeration districts, recognizing the significance of location in interpreting census data.

2. **Reservation and Off-Reservation Counts**: Understand the variations in counting indigenous populations living on and off reservations.

Contextualizing Data with Historical Events

1. **Impact of Events**: Examine how historical events, such as removals, relocations, and cultural shifts, influence the presence of American Indian populations in census records.
2. **Data Validation**: Validate census data by cross-referencing with other sources, recognizing discrepancies, and acknowledging the challenges of enumeration.

Indigenous Families in Census Records

1. **Familial Relationships**: Interpret census records to understand family structures, living arrangements, and relationships within indigenous households.
2. **Native Language Indicators**: Recognize how language proficiency indicators can provide insights into cultural practices and native languages spoken.

Crafting a Comprehensive Narrative

1. **Quantitative and Qualitative Analysis**: Combine quantitative data analysis with qualitative insights from historical context and oral histories to craft a comprehensive narrative.

2. **Collaboration with Tribal Communities**: Engage with tribal members and communities to interpret census data in the context of their histories and experiences.

Modern Census Considerations

1. **Self-Identification**: Understand the importance of self-identification in modern census data and its impact on accurately capturing American Indian populations.
2. **Advocacy for Inclusion**: Recognize the efforts of American Indian communities to ensure accurate enumeration and representation in modern censuses.

As we navigate the complexities of census data, we embrace the realization that census records, while imperfect, still hold valuable insights into the history and presence of American Indian populations. By decoding these records within historical and cultural contexts, we illuminate the lives of our ancestors and continue to shape the evolving narrative of indigenous heritage.

PIECES OF THE PUZZLE: DOCUMENTING THE DAWES ERA

Introduction

The Dawes Act of 1887 marked a pivotal period in American Indian history, leading to the creation of the Dawes Rolls—a valuable resource for genealogists tracing American Indian ancestry. In this chapter, we embark on a journey through the Dawes era, exploring the significance of the Dawes Rolls and uncovering the stories held within these documents.

The Dawes Act and Its Impact

1. **The Dawes Act Overview**: Understand the objectives and consequences of the Dawes Act, including land allotment and the transition to individual land ownership.
2. **Impact on Tribal Land**: Recognize the implications of land allotment on tribal land holdings, cultural practices, and indigenous communities.

The Dawes Commission and Enrollment Process

1. **Establishment of the Dawes Commission**: Learn about the creation of the Dawes Commission and its role in enrolling American Indian individuals.

2. **Enrollment Criteria and Process**: Explore the criteria used by the Dawes Commission to determine eligibility for enrollment, including blood quantum and tribal affiliation.

The Dawes Rolls: A Genealogical Treasure

1. **Contents of the Rolls**: Understand the information recorded in the Dawes Rolls, including names, ages, gender, tribal affiliations, and family relationships.
2. **Rolls as Historical Snapshots**: Recognize the Dawes Rolls as snapshots of American Indian families during a specific period, reflecting demographic changes.

Accessing and Navigating the Rolls

1. **Online and Offline Resources**: Explore online databases, archives, and repositories that provide access to the Dawes Rolls and related documents.
2. **Interpreting Codes and Annotations**: Understand the codes and annotations used in the rolls to identify familial relationships, tribal affiliations, and other details.

Challenges and Considerations

1. **Missed Connections**: Address the limitations of the Dawes Rolls, which may have missed individuals due to various factors, including cultural practices.
2. **Inaccuracies and Variations**: Navigate discrepancies and variations in names, spellings, and tribal affiliations within the Dawes Rolls.

Historical Context of Enrollment

1. **Family Disputes and Enrollments**: Explore cases where family disputes, estrangements, and disagreements affected enrollment decisions.
2. **Mixed-Race Families**: Understand the complexities faced by mixed-race families during the Dawes era and the implications for enrollment.

Legacy of the Dawes Era

1. **Impact on Identity**: Examine how the Dawes Rolls shaped perceptions of American Indian identity and the challenges faced by those not enrolled.
2. **Cultural Implications**: Recognize the cultural implications of enrollment, including the tension between traditional practices and the requirements of the Dawes Commission.

Using the Dawes Rolls as a Genealogical Tool

1. **Cross-Referencing with Other Records**: Explore how the Dawes Rolls can be cross-referenced with other documents to validate information and uncover additional details.
2. **Creating Family Trees**: Learn how to incorporate Dawes Rolls information into your family tree, tracing lineage and relationships.

The Dawes Rolls hold a wealth of information about American Indian families during a critical period of transformation. As we navigate this era, we gain insights not only into individual genealogies but also into the broader historical context that shaped the lives of our ancestors. By uncovering the stories within the Dawes Rolls, we pay homage to the resilience of those who lived through this era and continue to celebrate their legacies.

NAVIGATING THE ENIGMA OF BLOOD QUANTUM AND IDENTITY

Introduction

The concept of blood quantum, a measure of an individual's indigenous ancestry, has played a complex role in determining tribal membership and identity within American Indian communities. In this chapter, we delve into the intricate nuances of blood quantum, its historical context, and the challenges it poses to tracing American Indian ancestry.

Origins and Evolution of Blood Quantum

1. **Colonial Origins**: Explore the origins of blood quantum within the colonial context and its role in early interactions between indigenous populations and European settlers.
2. **Government Policies**: Understand how blood quantum became enmeshed in federal policies, affecting land allotments, tribal recognition, and legal definitions.

Calculating Blood Quantum

1. **Fractional Measurements**: Learn how blood quantum is often expressed as a fractional measurement, indicating the proportion of indigenous ancestry.

2. **Interpreting Generations**: Explore the complexity of calculating blood quantum over multiple generations and the challenges it presents.

Blood Quantum as a Criterion for Tribal Membership

1. **Membership Criteria**: Recognize how some tribes use blood quantum as a criterion for determining tribal enrollment and citizenship.
2. **Challenges of Inclusion and Exclusion**: Understand the delicate balance between preserving cultural identity and potentially excluding individuals with partial indigenous heritage.

Critiques and Debates

1. **Cultural Implications**: Explore how blood quantum can impact cultural practices and the perception of authenticity within indigenous communities.
2. **Erosion of Identity**: Understand concerns about the erosion of identity as individuals with higher blood quantum often experience difficulties in tracing roots.

Alternatives to Blood Quantum

1. **Cultural Affiliation**: Learn about alternative methods of tribal enrollment that prioritize cultural affiliation, community involvement, and commitment.
2. **Lineage and Identity**: Understand how some tribes emphasize lineage and connection to community rather than rigid blood quantum thresholds.

Documenting and Validating Ancestral Connections

1. **Tribal Enrollment Records**: Explore how tribal enrollment records often include information about blood quantum, family relationships, and tribal affiliations.
2. **Challenges in Historical Records**: Understand the difficulty of accurately determining blood quantum through historical records due to gaps, inaccuracies, and cultural complexities.

Ethical Considerations and Cultural Sensitivity

1. **Navigating Complexities**: Address the ethical considerations of discussing blood quantum and identity, respecting the sensitivities of indigenous communities.

2. **Understanding Individual Experiences**: Recognize that each individual's experience with blood quantum is unique and influenced by cultural, historical, and personal factors.

Identity Beyond Blood Quantum

1. **Cultural Continuity**: Understand the importance of cultural continuity and connection to community as integral aspects of American Indian identity.
2. **Shifting Perspectives**: Embrace the evolving perspectives on blood quantum and identity as tribes adapt to changing circumstances while preserving traditions.

As we navigate the enigma of blood quantum and identity, we recognize the complexities of this measure within the broader context of American Indian genealogy. By engaging with sensitivity and cultural awareness, we honor the diversity of indigenous experiences and the multifaceted ways in which individuals connect with their ancestral heritage.

ILLUMINATING ANCESTRAL THREADS: DNA QUEST IN AMERICAN INDIAN ANCESTRY

Advancements in genetic technology have opened new avenues for exploring ancestral connections, even in the realm of American Indian genealogy. DNA testing offers a unique lens through which we can peer into the past and uncover hidden threads of indigenous heritage. In this chapter, we embark on a genetic journey, exploring the benefits, challenges, and ethical considerations of using DNA testing to trace American Indian ancestry.

Genetic Genealogy and its Possibilities

1. **Genetic Inheritance**: Understand the basics of genetic inheritance and how specific markers are passed down through generations.
2. **DNA Testing Types**: Explore the different types of DNA testing—autosomal, mitochondrial, and Y-DNA—and their applications in genealogy.

Benefits of DNA Testing

1. **Breaking Down Brick Walls**: Learn how DNA testing can help overcome genealogical roadblocks and bridge gaps in documentary records.

2. **Confirmation of Lineages**: Understand how DNA testing can confirm documented lineages and connect distant relatives.

Native American DNA and Challenges

1. **Distinct Genetic Patterns**: Recognize the unique genetic markers and patterns associated with Native American ancestry, which can aid identification.
2. **Limited Representation**: Address the challenge of limited genetic samples from specific tribes, leading to varying levels of accuracy.

DNA Testing Companies and Tools

1. **Popular Testing Companies**: Explore the major DNA testing companies and their databases, which may contain information relevant to American Indian ancestry.
2. **Third-Party Tools**: Discover third-party tools and platforms that offer advanced analysis and tools for genealogical research.

Interpreting DNA Results

1. **Ethnicity Estimates**: Understand the limitations of ethnicity estimates and their role in providing a broad overview of ancestral origins.
2. **Matching Relatives**: Learn how to interpret DNA matches, identifying potential relatives and determining their relationships.

Navigating Ethical Considerations

1. **Informed Consent**: Recognize the importance of informed consent when sharing DNA data and connecting with potential relatives.
2. **Cultural Sensitivity**: Understand the ethical considerations of using DNA testing within indigenous communities, respecting cultural beliefs and practices.

Collaborative Research and Community Involvement

1. **Tribe-Specific Projects**: Engage with DNA projects focused on specific tribes, fostering collaboration and sharing genetic data.
2. **Community Outreach**: Explore efforts to involve indigenous communities in DNA research, ensuring their voices are heard and respected.

Unveiling Hidden Connections

1. **Unexpected Discoveries**: Acknowledge the potential for unexpected familial connections and the emotional impact of newfound relatives.
2. **Continuing the Quest**: Understand that DNA testing is a complement to traditional research, offering new insights while honoring existing genealogical methods.

Preserving Cultural Identity

1. **Integration of DNA and Culture**: Embrace the integration of DNA testing with cultural identity, recognizing that it is one facet of a multifaceted heritage.
2. **Celebrating Shared Ancestry**: Embrace the potential for DNA testing to foster connections between individuals with shared indigenous heritage.

DNA testing offers a window into the complex tapestry of American Indian ancestry, providing a bridge between generations and a pathway to uncovering hidden connections. As we embark on this DNA quest, we do so with a respect for cultural sensitivities, a commitment to collaboration, and an understanding that the stories revealed by genetic testing are only one layer of a broader narrative.

By weaving together the threads of documentary research, oral traditions, and genetic insights, we enrich our understanding of indigenous heritage and honor the legacies of our ancestors.

TRACING ROOTS THROUGH AMERICAN INDIAN ANCESTRY

The path to uncovering American Indian ancestry is a journey that intertwines genealogy with history, culture, and the complex tapestry of indigenous communities. In this chapter, we embark on an exploration of tracing American Indian roots, delving into the methods, resources, and considerations essential for this endeavor.

Genealogical Landmarks in Indigenous Communities

1. **Tribal Histories**: Recognize the importance of understanding the histories, migrations, and cultural practices of specific tribes to aid in tracing ancestry.
2. **Cultural Signifiers**: Learn to identify cultural markers, such as names, clans, and affiliations, that can provide genealogical clues.

Consulting Tribal Elders and Knowledge Keepers

1. **Cultural Traditions**: Explore the role of tribal elders and knowledge keepers as repositories of historical and genealogical information.

2. **Approaching with Respect**: Understand the cultural protocols and respect required when seeking guidance from tribal elders and community members.

Accessing Tribal Resources and Archives

1. **Tribal Archives**: Learn how tribal archives, libraries, and cultural centers house valuable records and documents for genealogical research.
2. **Oral Histories and Record Keepers**: Discover the significance of oral traditions and designated record keepers within tribal communities.

Triangulating Oral Traditions and Records

1. **Blending Oral and Written**: Understand how combining oral narratives with documented records can provide a more comprehensive understanding of ancestral history.
2. **Contextual Interpretation**: Learn to interpret oral histories within the cultural and historical contexts of specific tribes and communities.

Tribal Enrollment and Membership Records

1. **Tribal Enrollment Applications**: Explore how tribal enrollment records provide information about ancestral connections and family relationships.
2. **Respecting Privacy**: Understand the importance of respecting the privacy and protocols surrounding tribal enrollment records.

Federal Records and Government Documents

1. **Bureau of Indian Affairs Records**: Learn how records from the Bureau of Indian Affairs contain information about land allotments, annuities, and more.
2. **Dawes Rolls and Beyond**: Understand the significance of the Dawes Rolls and similar records in documenting tribal affiliations and family relationships.

DNA Testing and Tribal Affiliation

1. **DNA and Tribal Connections**: Explore how DNA testing can complement genealogical research by providing insights into ancestral connections.
2. **Community DNA Projects**: Learn about DNA projects within tribal communities and the importance of community consent and involvement.

Cultural Sensitivity and Collaborative Efforts

1. **Ethical Research**: Navigate genealogical research with cultural sensitivity, considering the implications of accessing sacred or sensitive information.
2. **Collaborating with Tribes**: Embrace collaborative research with tribal members, contributing to the collective understanding of genealogy and history.

Celebrating Shared Heritage

1. **Connecting to Community**: Recognize the sense of belonging that comes from uncovering and celebrating shared heritage within tribal communities.
2. **Resilience and Continuity**: Understand that tracing American Indian ancestry is a testament to the resilience of indigenous cultures and the continuity of traditions.

As we navigate the intricate landscape of tracing American Indian ancestry, we do so with reverence for the cultures, histories, and traditions that have shaped indigenous communities. By combining genealogical methods with cultural respect and collaboration, we not only piece together individual family stories but contribute to the broader narrative of indigenous heritage.

THE LONG WALK FORWARD: PRESERVING AND SHARING DISCOVERIES

As the culmination of your journey to trace American Indian ancestry, the path doesn't conclude with research alone—it extends into the crucial steps of preserving and sharing your invaluable discoveries. In this chapter, we embark on the long walk forward, navigating the intricate terrain of documenting your findings, crafting a family history, and contributing to the broader narrative of American Indian genealogy.

Capturing Your Ancestral Journey

1. **Organizing Your Research**: Learn effective techniques to organize and catalog your research materials, creating a structured foundation for your discoveries.

2. **Digitizing Documents and Records**: Understand the significance of digitizing paper documents and photographs, preserving them for generations to come.

Crafting a Living Family History

1. **Weaving the Threads of Storytelling**: Transform your research into a compelling family history, interweaving

genealogical facts with cultural context and personal anecdotes.

2. **Visual Enhancements**: Explore the impact of incorporating visual elements like maps, photographs, and documents to enhance the richness of your narrative.

Preserving Physical Treasures

1. **Photographic Preservation**: Discover methods to safeguard aging photographs, ensuring that their stories endure for future generations.

2. **Conserving Heirlooms and Artifacts**: Explore techniques to preserve cherished objects, documents, and textiles, connecting the past with the present.

Digital Archives and Safekeeping

1. **Digital Backup Strategies**: Understand the importance of creating digital backups and utilizing cloud storage to protect your digital genealogical assets.

2. **Online Genealogy Repositories**: Explore online repositories and platforms that allow you to securely share your research while contributing to the larger genealogy community.

Sharing the Rich Heritage

1. **Family Gatherings and Reunions**: Embrace family gatherings as opportune moments to share your findings, fostering connections and sparking interest in ancestral stories.

2. **Contribution to Community**: Consider collaborating with local historical societies, cultural centers, or tribal archives to contribute to the broader narrative of American Indian genealogy.

Engaging the Future Generations

1. **Educational Endeavors**: Develop educational materials or workshops that captivate younger family members, igniting their passion for genealogical exploration.

2. **Youth-Centric Outreach**: Discover creative ways to make genealogy appealing to the younger generation, drawing them into the rich tapestry of their heritage.

Ethical Considerations and Cultural Sensitivity

1. **Respecting Privacy**: Acknowledge the significance of safeguarding living relatives' privacy and gaining consent before sharing sensitive information.
2. **Cultural Protocols**: Navigate cultural protocols within American Indian communities, respecting traditions while sharing information that resonates.

Leaving a Legacy for Eternity

1. **Continuing the Quest**: Encourage family members to embark on their own genealogical journeys, ensuring that the flame of discovery continues to burn brightly.
2. **Staying Connected**: Embrace the potential of technology and social media to maintain connections and ensure the ongoing preservation of your ancestral legacy.

The long walk forward after research encompasses the preservation and sharing of your genealogical gems. Through this chapter, you'll cultivate an enduring tribute to the resilience, wisdom, and cultural heritage of your ancestors. As your legacy unfolds, it bridges generations, nurtures a sense of identity, and fosters unity— illuminating the path for those who follow in your footsteps.

CONCLUSION: EMBRACING THE ANCESTRAL PATHWAY

As we reach the end of this ancestral journey, I invite you to pause and reflect on the significance of the path you've traversed. Your exploration of American Indian ancestry has led you through a landscape rich with stories, histories, and connections that resonate across generations. Through the labyrinth of research, the weaving of narratives, and the preservation of heritage, you've engaged with a legacy that extends far beyond the confines of time.

Embracing the Tapestry of Heritage

By delving into your American Indian heritage, you've not only uncovered ancestral roots but also woven threads that connect you to a multifaceted tapestry of identity. Your ancestors' stories are a testament to their resilience, wisdom, and the myriad ways in which they shaped their communities, even in the face of adversity. As you embrace this tapestry, you become a living embodiment of the diverse experiences that have defined your family's narrative.

A Power in Belonging

Through this journey, you've realized that belonging is not confined to a single moment or place—it's a power that echoes through time, forging connections that defy boundaries. Your American Indian heritage is a source of strength, resilience, and continuity that spans generations, creating a bridge between past, present, and future. It's a reminder that you are part of something larger than yourself—a living legacy that continues to evolve.

Continuing the Discovery

As this chapter closes, let it serve as a prelude to the chapters yet unwritten. Your journey of discovery is far from over—it is a dynamic, ongoing process that evolves as you learn, share, and connect. The stories of your ancestors will continue to inspire and guide you, encouraging you to delve deeper, explore wider, and celebrate the heritage that courses through your veins.

Celebrating Resilience and Belonging

In embracing your American Indian heritage, you've embraced a story of resilience, belonging, and the enduring spirit of your ancestors. Let your journey serve as a reminder that your identity is multi-dimensional, shaped by a rich tapestry of cultures, histories, and traditions. As you celebrate this heritage, you honor the stories that have shaped your family, and you contribute to a broader narrative that celebrates the diversity and unity of the American Indian experience.

Beyond These Pages

As you close this book, remember that your journey does not conclude here. It continues through the connections you foster, the stories you share, and the bridges you build. Your American Indian heritage is a living legacy—one that you hold in your heart, carry in your actions, and pass down to future generations. Embrace this ancestral pathway with pride, for it is a journey of discovery that knows no end.

May your journey be filled with continued discovery, renewed connections, and the profound understanding that you are a part of a vibrant and enduring tapestry—a tapestry that spans both time and place, forever connecting you to the power of your American Indian heritage.

The End.

www.ingramcontent.com/pod-product-compliance
Lightning Source LLC
Chambersburg PA
CBHW060259030426
42335CB00014B/1769